D1359558

The Beauty of
KENYA

Mohamed Amin · Duncan Willetts

Text Book Centre

This edition published 1993 by
Text Book Centre Ltd.
Kijabe Street,
P.O. Box 47540
Nairobi
Kenya

First published 1984

Second Impression 1985
Third Impression 1989
Fourth Impression 1993

© Camerapix 1984

ISBN 1 874041 36 9

This book was designed and produced by
Camerapix Publishers International
P. O. Box 45048, Nairobi, Kenya

Printed in Hong Kong by South China Printing Co.

*Half-title: Samburu maiden and warrior. Title page: Turkana
men in the Suguta Valley. Contents page: Reticulated giraffes on
Laikipia Plains beneath 17,058 foot high Mount Kenya which sits
astride the Equator.*

Contents

Previous pages: Diani Beach, one of Kenya's many fine coast resorts.

Below left: Luo dancer. Bottom left: Merille fisherman, Lake Turkana. Below right: Rendille woman, Kaisut desert. Bottom right: Bok woman carrying traditional water pitcher.

Introduction

For the visitor nurtured on the writings of Rider Haggard, Ernest Hemingway, Karen Blixen, Elspeth Huxley, Robert Ruark, Jim Corbett, Baden-Powell, Joy Adamson, and the celluloid epics of the golden years of Hollywood, Kenya has always exerted a magic spell.

This nation at the heart of a great continent has remained a more powerful magnet for tourists from the Western world than any other country in Black Africa.

And it's easy to see why. Kenya is scenically magnificent; 583,644 square kilometres (225,345 square miles), much of it dramatic wilderness unsurpassed anywhere in the world.

Straddling the Equator and riven down its middle by the Great Rift Valley, Kenya's landscapes are varied and beautiful opposites—from snow-capped mountain peak to blazing desert, from rain-soaked timber forest to glistening white beaches. And studded throughout the land are more than 40 wildlife parks and reserves which contain some of the world's most interesting wildlife species.

Kenya is also exceptional in other ways than the ageless wonder of its scenery and wildlife. The country's history since 1963, when independence was won from the British, under the leadership of freedom fighter "Mzee" Jomo Kenyatta, is one of remarkable social and economic advances. Symbolic of Kenya's success in merging traditional Africa tribal society with modern technological society is the imposing Kenyatta International Conference Centre in the heart of Nairobi. The Centre's 30-storey tower is Kenya's most imposing building; the cone-shaped roof of its amphitheatre inspired by the traditional African round hut. A statue of Kenya's founding father, Jomo Kenyatta, who died in 1978, stands in the Centre's forecourt.

Opposite top: Kenyatta Avenue, Nairobi's main street. This modern capital was born on 30 May 1899.

Opposite bottom: Kenya's ultra-modern Jomo Kenyatta International Airport at Nairobi, headquarters of the national flag carrier, Kenya Airways.

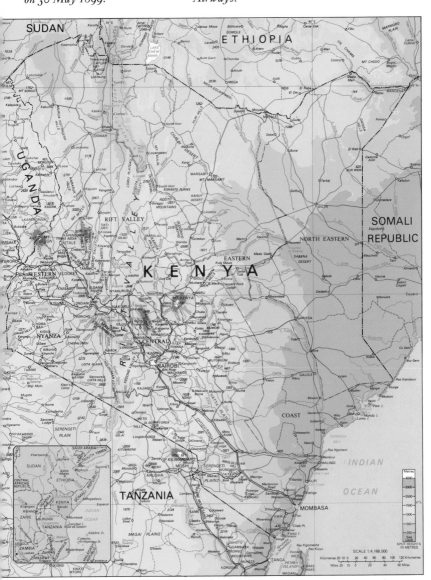

"Green City in the Sun"

At the centre of harp-shaped Kenya is the capital, Nairobi, a city of about a million people. Despite Nairobi's size and modernity, however, it is the pungent smell of earth and flowers and the extraordinary clarity of light which first strikes the visitor here on the Equator, a mile (1,670 metres) above sea level.

This "green city in the sun" is a mosaic of woodland and pleasant parks, winding lanes and broad highways, mansions and shanties, industrial sites and well-kept lawns.

The trees of the outer suburbs clothe the city in a luxuriant green shawl, patterned by houses of many styles and vintages, with gardens ablaze with the colour of shrubs and flowers that thrive in the year-round equable, temperate climate. Trees and green spaces in the city centre soften the harsh concrete outlines of modern hotels and geometric office buildings, cinemas, night clubs, art galleries and government buildings. Among Nairobi's groves and forest patches are open golf courses, the testing chicanes of a motor race track, the green oblong of the city's Ngong horse-racing course, a polo ground and the show stands and arena of Jamhuri Park. This agricultural and industrial display park, set amidst indigenous forest, is often described as the world's most beautiful showground. Annually it presents the Nairobi International Show—shop-window for Kenya's long-established agriculture and mushrooming industry.

Dinghies and sailboats glide across the dark, reed-fringed waters of Nairobi Dam, a postwar man-made lake, flanked on one side by new middle-class housing estates and the tin-and-wood shanty town of Kibera. And on yet another side is Wilson Airport, base for

Overleaf: Verdant grass, crowded grandstand and a close finish at Nairobi's Ngong Racecourse run by the Jockey Club of Kenya.

hundreds of Kenya's light aircraft, mostly owned by charter firms which do a booming business to destinations within Kenya and far beyond. In terms of its take-offs and landings, it is one of Africa's busiest airfields. Beyond Wilson Airport, to the south-east of the city's urban sprawl, is a triangular wedge of wilderness—Nairobi National Park. It is made up of 110 square kilometres (42 square miles) of plains and forest with its eastern apex touching the satellite town of Athi River. Home for many forms of wildlife, the park is separated from the bustle of Nairobi's flour mills, tyre plants, vehicle assembly shops, breweries, plastics factories and pharmaceutical enterprises by a mere wire fence.

Near the city centre, rail tracks loop and curve into a great maze of marshalling yards. It was here, on 30 May, 1899, that Nairobi was born on a bare, flat plain at the edge of a papyrus swamp, when the builders of the Uganda Railway—"The Lunatic Line"—paused to establish a supply depot before embarking on the difficult climb to the edge of the Great Rift Valley's eastern wall, nearly 8,000 feet (2,438 metres) above sea level.

Nairobi soon became a sprawling, squalid, fever-ridden bazaar shanty of hovels and lean-tos, frenetic with 24-hour-a-day activity. But that temporary railhead base now is an elegant capital city covering 698 square kilometres (269 square miles). From its beginning, Nairobi always contained a polyglot, cosmopolitan community. The thousands of immigrants who flocked to Kenya in the wake of the railway's arrival brought with them their own cultures, a heritage that has helped to make today's Kenya truly multi-racial. As recently as September 1983 an African electorate

overwhelmingly returned a white Kenyan as their Member of Parliament for Nairobi's Langata constituency—and a large proportion of Asian Kenyans voted for a veteran African politician in the city's Parklands constituency.

Nairobi has become known world-wide as the gateway to adventure and safaris. In English, the word safari originally meant "a hunting expedition". Its contemporary usage, however, goes far beyond the Oxford English Dictionary's generic definition. The word has come to suggest the romance and excitement of leaving city and towns far behind, of entering virgin bush crowded with animals of all shapes and descriptions under an azure-blue sky, flecked with cotton-wool clouds. It no longer means only killing wild animals; most visitors are now content with photographing them.

Yet a safari in most senses of the word is possible without even leaving Nairobi. Only eight kilometres (five miles) from Parliament Buildings and the Kenyatta International Conference Centre lies Nairobi National Park, the country's first wildlife reserve, which opened in 1946. (Fifty years after all of what was then "Kenia District" had been proclaimed a game reserve). At night the Park's lions break the stillness with their sonorous roars. Small game and monkeys frequently raid vegetable patches and poke around the shrubs and compost heaps of homes in Nairobi's outskirts. Occasionally larger animals stray from the Park; in 1984 a leopard was seen in a crowded modern Nairobi estate close to the city centre, sneaking around the walls of a maisonette. In 1956 a lion had to be shot when it strayed out of the Park and finally ended up

in the garden of a private residence less than a mile from the heart of Nairobi. Inside the Park gates the transition from today to the former wild Africa is sudden: a journey back in both time and space. The Park is unchanged by man's forces, its seasons recurring in a pageant of primal and pristine Africa as it has for thousands of years. Yet clearly visible from within the park is Nairobi's familiar serried skyline.

The only major wildlife species the Park does not contain is elephant. Buffalo and rhino disappeared after the turn of the century—the plains on which the Park stands provided an ideal location for the new town's hunting buffs to indulge in blood-letting. However, the two species were re-introduced successfully in the 1960s.

At the Park's main entrance is the Nairobi Animal Orphanage, established as a rehabilitation and rescue centre for orphans from the wild. Some animals that cannot be returned to their natural homes have become permanent residents. Sebastian, its greatest character, is a chain-smoking chimpanzee whose antics over the years have entertained thousands. He has a renowned temper, especially if deprived of his beloved nicotine. On many occasions he has outwitted his captors and escaped into the nearby forests, disappearing up the tallest trees. The only way to capture him is with an anaesthetic dart but once he went to sleep before the safety net was strung up beneath him. He thumped to the ground with a bone-jarring jolt, fortunately without damage.

Opposite top: Cheetah family taking water in Nairobi National Park. Opposite bottom: Pair of rare black rhinoceros.

Below: Susua Volcano's inner plateau, a 'lost world' in Kenya's Rift Valley. The Aberdares and Mount Kenya rise above the horizon.

Heartland of Kenya

In the background, west of Nairobi Park, stand the Ngong Hills, a knuckle-shaped ridge of forested peaks which form part of the eastern wall of the Great Rift Valley.

The highest point touches more than 8,000 feet (2,438 metres), but the hump-back slopes are gentle and easy for walking. From the top there are magnificent views over the Rift Valley with its scarps, cliffs and extinct volcanoes. The lower slopes on the east of the hills are now extensively cultivated by peasant smallholders. The Ngongs were beloved by Karen Blixen, who wrote the classic *Out of Africa* under her literary alias of Isak Dinesen.

To the west of the Ngong Hills, down on the Rift floor, is Olorgasailie, where prehistoric remains were first noted in 1890 by John Walter Gregory—the man who named the eastern fork of the Great Rift Valley. Later the site was excavated and described by the great palaeontologists, Drs Louis and Mary Leakey. Further down the valley, baking all the year round in the inferno of the Rift Valley floor, is Lake Magadi. Shimmering white against the impressive backdrop of the game-rich Nkuruman Escarpment that forms part of the Rift's western wall, the lake's trona deposits are second only in size to California's Salton Sea.

Assayed by Gregory in the 1890s, the trona was first exploited in 1911, and now the soda ash from the deposits finds a ready market in Africa and south-east Asia. This mother lode of mineral wealth has established such a lucrative base that a self-contained company town has sprung up on the lake's shore. Rich in birdlife, particularly waders and flamingo, Magadi is a "Dante's Inferno" burnt dry by the heat, but with an appeal that lures visitors back

again and again.

Just over 50 kilometres (30 miles) to the south-east of Nairobi is the agricultural town of Machakos, capital of Ukambani, the land of the Kamba people. The town's name is an Anglicised corruption of a Kamba elder's name—Masaku—who held authority before and during the time the trade caravans walked up from the coast into the interior. The town is ringed by delightful hills producing abundant crops of fruit and vegetables after good rains. The Kamba people, traditionally hunters, have developed a reputation as fine soldiers, policemen and wood carvers in more recent times.

Not far from Machakos to the north is Ukambani's coffee town of Kangundo and nearby Tala, known for its colourful, twice-weekly market. Northwards from Tala is the smooth rounded dome of ol Doinyo Sapuk—a hill known to the Kamba as *Kilimambogo*, and now a national park. Three lonely tombstones halfway up ol Doinyo Sapuk mark the graves of Sir William Northrup McMillan, his wife and their faithful servant, Louis Decker. Sir William, who fought with the British forces during the First World War, was one of the few Americans ever knighted by the British.

A road runs north-west from ol Doinyo Sapuk across the Athi, second largest of Kenya's easterly-flowing rivers. Near this crossing, the Athi River cascades over lips of rock known as Fourteen Falls to create a vista of enduring beauty. Beyond the Athi the road curves into Thika, the coffee growers' centre, vividly recorded in Elspeth Huxley's childhood autobiography, *The Flame Trees of Thika*. In 1907 Winston Churchill stayed at the Blue Posts

22

Left : Tracks and pipelines run across the soda crust surface of Lake Magadi in Kenya's Southern Rift Valley where trona is dredged and processed for glass production.

Below: Cabbages for sale in Tala Market, near Machakos.

Hotel, which still stands overlooking both the Chania and Thika Falls, and hunted lions nearby. Now an industrial satellite of Nairobi, Thika is a thriving town with fruit and vegetable canning, textile, tanning and milling industries, and a large car assembly plant.

It stands astride Kenya's "Great North Road" to Ethiopia. Many smaller roads descend from the high foothills of the Aberdares and Mount Kenya to link up the crowded settlements and farmlands of the Kikuyu people with this "Great North Road". Murang'a is the major town of the eastern Aberdare watershed. Once known as Fort Hall—after Major Francis Hall the British administrator who built a fort there around the turn of the century—it lies atop a hillside which plunges steep to the roaring floodwaters of the north Mathioya river, one of many tributaries of the Tana, Kenya's largest river.

From Murang'a a modern road to Othaya and Nyeri provides scenery of incomparable beauty as it criss-crosses some of the richest and best cultivated farmland in Kenya. Tidy, well-kept smallholdings on the higher ridges produce much of the tea grown in Kenya, together with other smallholdings on the slopes of Mount Kenya to the east.

Nyeri, a hill town on the slopes of the Aberdares (now also known as the Nyandarua) overlooking the Laikipia Plains, was once on the edge of Maasai territory and the Kikuyu farming area. It, too, is an important agricultural centre, and also a base from which to enter the Aberdare National Park, with its network of mountain roads at well over 10,000 feet (3,048 metres). Among the

town's several hotels is the rambling, spacious Outspan which the founder of the world-wide Boy Scout movement, Lord Robert Baden-Powell, chose as his retirement home. The cottage in which Lord Baden-Powell spent the last years of his life, "Paxtu", is a living museum to his memory, still used as a suite by Outspan guests.

Though an old warrior, Lord Baden-Powell was a seeker after peace—hence the name "Paxtu", deriving from the Latin "pax" and the Swahili "tu" meaning "only". It was also a pun, for his house in Britain was named Pax One. Baden-Powell lies buried in Nyeri churchyard. He always believed that "the nearer to Nyeri, the nearer to Heaven".

Nyeri today is the busy provincial capital of Central Province, populated almost entirely by Kikuyu living on the fertile ridges which lead off the Aberdare Mountains all the way from Kiambu, on the northern outskirts of Nairobi. The Kikuyu are the largest tribe in Kenya, closely allied by custom and language to the Embu to the south-east and the Meru, to the north-east. Today large numbers of Kikuyu also farm in the Rift Valley, and they are prominent in business enterprises throughout the country, as well as in Nairobi itself.

Kikuyu society is built around the family, often a large and extended unit, and the tribe's nine clans. Though women labour in the fields as well as in the houses, they are far from downtrodden. Mothers guide their husbands and sons with sound advice and chastising tongues. They inculcate the girls into the ways of womanhood. Polygamy is natural, often loving.

Below: Coffee plantation in the fertile Aberdare foothills at Nyeri. Kenya's arabica species earns high prices internationally.

Opposite: Athi River cascades over Fourteen Falls near Thika with forested slopes of ol Doinyo Sapuk National Park in background.

Goats are killed to propitiate tribal spirits, to remove curses and to provide omens for the future. These are the occasions, often festive, when the honey beer—*muratina*—is brewed. The container is set on a small pile of cattle dung, by the glowing embers of the day's fire. Roots from various bushes and succulents, and the fruit of the *muratina* tree, which looks like a loofah, are fermented in a large vessel with honey, sugar and water. By tradition the beer is poured from a gourd into a cow horn and passed around a circle of men. The women sit elsewhere. It is a formal, rigidly-observed ritual.

Near Nyeri is Treetops, a game-viewing hideaway in the Aberdare Forest. Built high up in a tree by Eric Sherbrook Walker in Peter Pan style to please his wife, Treetops has a permanent niche in the history of Britain's monarchy. It was here that Princess Elizabeth, descending on 6 February, 1952, from a night of game watching, learned she had become Britain's Queen upon her father's death during the night. Almost thirty-two years later (13 November, 1983) she renewed her unique links with Kenya during a five-day State visit when she made a brief, sentimental return to Treetops.

The real beauty of the Aberdares lies high above Nyeri and its thickly-forested skirt. Above the forests at between 10,000 and 12,000 feet (3,000 and 3,500 metres), runs a 46-kilometre (28 miles) long moorland plateau, marked at its northern extremity by ol Doinyo Lesatima, 13,120 feet (4,000 metres) high and in the south by the Kinangop, 12,700 feet (3,900 metres).

Aberdare National Park, running the length of these high

moorlands, is one of Kenya's oldest and most enchanting National Parks. Studded with giant heather and tussock grass, giant lobelias and groundsel (*senecio*), it is not only unforgettable, but genuinely breathtaking. Lungs labour for oxygen at such altitudes. The spoor of wild animals, both predator and prey, are often visible. Human visitors are infrequent and the animals display little fear of them. The rivers are crystal clear and icy cold, often interrupted by spectacular waterfalls. Only a brisk walk from the road are falls where the Gura River plummets almost 1,000 feet (300 metres) in three steps, its waters swaying like plastic thread in the wind, but always unerringly hitting the same spot below.

Despite the cold (the temperatures frequently fall below freezing at night) there are many animals on the Aberdare moorlands; forest elephant and buffalo, stately eland, and the shy bongo, also duiker, waterbuck, lion, leopard, colobus monkey and serval cat. The leopards and servals living in these high altitudes often have black coats instead of the normal sandy-coloured background, bestrewn with black spots.

Running the length of the Aberdare Range along its western flank and below the forests is the flat, heavily-farmed, Kinangop plateau. The southernmost reaches of this plateau drain into the Sasumua Dam, one of Nairobi's largest sources of water and still an idyllic fishing spot.

Midway along the plateau rises Kipipiri, an isolated often black and brooding peak wraithed in rain cloud. The mountain is separated from the main massif of the Aberdares by the Wanjohi Valley—once known as "Happy Valley"—for between the two

Below: Queen Elizabeth's historic return with Prince Philip on 13 November 1983 to the Aberdares water hole where she became Queen in 1952. Hunter Dick Prickett shows her around the old Treetops site with the new lodge in the background.

Opposite: Guinea fowl struts among magnificent Bongo, a nocturnal forest antelope of the Aberdares.

Opposite left: Crowned Crane. Opposite right: An exotic species of Crane at Mount Kenya Safari Club.

World Wars it was notorious for the high jinks of a group of fast and loose-living white settlers. This remote valley is now farmed by Kikuyu and the stately mansions which once echoed to the sounds of hectic parties at which guests were served the finest champagne by liveried retainers are now deserted, inhabited only by goats, cattle, chickens and the ghosts of yesteryear. No longer are the ostrich races a regular attraction. All effort is now directed to making a living from the fertile soil.

To the north of the Aberdares the grassy Laikipia Plains disappear into a seemingly infinite expanse of African savanna. Eighty kilometres (50 miles) to the east, the twin spires of Mount Kenya—Batian at 17,058 feet (5200 metres) and Nelion, just 30 feet (10 metres) or so lower—thrust into the azure tropical sky. They take their names, as does a third peak—Lenana—from three famous Maasai medicine men or *laibons*.

Water pours off the eastern and southern slopes of Mount Kenya and merges with streams from the Aberdares to form the Tana River, now the country's main source of hydro-electricity. A succession of dams along the Tana's upper course diverts water through turbines which fuel Kenya's hydro-electrical system. The oldest of these man-made lakes, Kindaruma, is 46 kilometres (over 28 miles) long and besides serving as the base of a growing fisheries industry, it makes a convenient weekend resort for Nairobi residents. Another, Masinga Lake, is almost 80 kilometres (50 miles) long and forms the largest man-made sheet of water in East Africa, but will soon have a rival in the adjacent Kiambere Dam when completed.

The rivers flowing off south-eastern Mount Kenya also irrigate the Mwea rice fields. The thousands of acres of flooded paddies lure many waterfowl, whose presence gladdens the bird lover's heart, but saddens the rice farmers, as they destroy the young rice shoots.

The District Headquarters of Embu, above the Mwea Plains, serve a large farming community on the lower slopes of Mount Kenya. The town is graced by a pleasant English-style hostelry— the Isaac Walton Inn—widely used by anglers who come to catch trout from the streams running off Mount Kenya.

From Embu a road circles Mount Kenya's base. The northern arc goes through Meru, a town of 70,000. This is a friendly, industrious community of agriculturalists on the higher ground and pastoralists in the hotter lowlands. Meru National Park, one of the most interesting in all Kenya, is famous because it was here, before the area was gazetted a park, that Joy and George Adamson rehabilitated their tame lion Elsa to the wild and inspired the best selling book *Born Free*. Today Joy is dead, tragically murdered, and George has moved downstream to the Kora Game Reserve, where he continues his association with lions into his ninth decade.

From Meru the round-Mount-Kenya-road heads north-west and then west, affording a magnificent panoramic view of Kenya's arid north. The humpbacks of dormant volcanoes protruding blue-grey out of the flat expanse vanish into far distant haze, heat shimmering below the cool mountain air.

The "Great North Road", traversing some of Kenya's most remote desert lands *en route* to the highlands of distant Ethiopia,

Opposite : Grevy's zebra in Samburu Reserve.

Right : Gerenuk, or giraffe-necked gazelle, in Samburu.

Right : Reticulated giraffe splays legs to take water. The world's tallest animal reaches 18 to 19 feet high.

Opposite : Nile crocodile feeding on bait on banks of the Ewaso Ngiro, Samburu Reserve.

also runs through Isiolo. This untidy, sprawling town is the main commercial centre for this perpetually drought-stricken land. Only a little way out into the dry lands from Isiolo lie three splendid game reserves—Samburu, Buffalo Springs and Shaba. All three lie along the northern Uaso Nyiro River that drains the northern slopes of the Aberdares and Mount Kenya, channelling its waters to waste in the distant Lorian Swamp, where they seep into the ground, or evaporate in the fierce heat.

These three game reserves exhibit fauna and flora typical of arid lands, perhaps best epitomised by the elegant gerenuk, an attractive species, also known as Waller's gazelle, which has adapted to life in the low, hot and dry Horn of Africa. Its third name—giraffe-necked gazelle—describes its physical appearance. The gerenuk's long legs and long neck enable it to browse on the tall acacia bushes and trees characteristic of the region. It has the unique ability to stand upright on its hindlegs, enabling it to reach high into the trees for precious greenery. Shaba Game Reserve has strong Adamson connections, for it was there that Joy Adamson released a cheetah to the wild and was preparing to do the same with a leopard when she was murdered by an ex-employee with a grudge.

South and westward from Isiolo the round-the-mountain-road, joins the "Great North Road" before climbing over the north-western shoulder of Mount Kenya, reaching the wheat farms of Timau. Here, at around 9,000 feet (2,740 metres) above sea level, wheat and wool are produced on a series of large estates. Beyond is the ranchers' town of Nanyuki, servicing the big spreads on the

Laikipia Plains. Here a large military base and airfield guards the northern approaches to Kenya's highlands. Nanyuki is also the site of the luxurious Mount Kenya Safari Club, with its nine-hole golf course, heated swimming pool and a members' list which includes many of the world's famous and wealthy. The club was the brainchild of an American oil millionaire, the late Ray Ryan, and some of his friends, including the late film star, William Holden. "Bill" Holden made his home on the game ranch just below the Club and found release from the pressures of fame and work by helping his partner, Don Hunt, in a game trapping business. He became a dedicated conservationist in the process, and a Wildlife Foundation has now been created in his memory.

South from Nanyuki, and heading back towards Nyeri, the round-the-mountain-road crosses the Naro Moru River and a hamlet of the same name. Naro Moru is the most frequently-used base for those climbing the snow-dusted peaks of Mount Kenya and its dozen glaciers. Mount Kenya National Park encompasses most of the mountain above 10,000 feet (3,030 metres). The main gate on the track from Naro Moru lies at 8,200 feet (2,500 metres) in a thick belt of bamboo forest, which gives way to thick stands of ancient trees festooned with Spanish moss before the moorlands break out at around 11,500 feet (3,500 metres) offering fine walks for the hardiest and fittest—beware of the "vertical bog" after the rains, lest you sink into the peaty morass. Even at 8,200 feet (2,500 metres) walking through the bamboo belt is like trudging through a humid oven—shirts quickly become drenched in sweat.

Thirty-two jewel-like lakes dot the radius of Mount Kenya's

Below: Colourful shrubs frame lush greenery of Mount Kenya Safari Club.

Opposite: Twelve thousand foot moorland ridge climbs to the base of 17,058 foot high Mount Kenya's snow-dusted twin peaks of Batian and Nelion (17,022 feet) divided by a knife-edge ridge, the 'Saddle of Mists'.

main peaks, and hundreds of secondary peaks offer challenges tough enough to test the most experienced Himalayan and Alpine specialists, with some of the most difficult and dangerous ice climbs in the world. The topmost peaks form the "plug" that rose out of Mount Kenya's volcano, and the rest has weathered away. It is estimated that at its prime, perhaps a million years ago, the peak stood at about 23,000 feet (7,000 metres) with a profile resembling Kilimanjaro, making it a giant among the world's mountains. It still remains Africa's second highest peak.

One of the few mountains on the Equator, it was not until the missionary, the Reverend Ludwig Krapf, saw the white-capped peaks from the east in 1849 that the ancient legends about its glaciers and snow were confirmed as fact. It is regarded as the most perfect model of an Equatorial mountain. Sir Halford MacKinder was the first to conquer its tallest peak, Batian, in 1899. Not until 1929 was it climbed again when Himalayan experts Eric Shipton and Wyn Harris became the next two men known to have stood atop Batian, 17,058 feet (5,199 metres).

These peaks were the subject of an unusual true-life drama recorded in the Italian book, *No Picnic on Mount Kenya*, which tells how three prisoners-of-war interned at Nanyuki during the 1940's tired of confinement, broke out of the camp to climb the mountain—with only the label on a tin of canned meat as a map. Hunger and the alpine weather overcame the runaways, whose poignant failure renders the account of their adventures more dramatic than success would have done. Their exploit over, they calmly returned to their camp to resume their confinement!

Back near Nyeri, the road passes through Kiganjo, where Kenya's Police College trains the force's recruits. From here you can head back to Nairobi via Murang'a and Thika, or in dry weather cross over the Aberdares' high, scenic saddle and drop down into the Rift at the farming town of Naivasha. Nearby Lake Naivasha is the purest of all Kenya's Rift Valley lakes and a convenient pleasure resort for Nairobi's residents. At weekends they arrive by the hundreds to fish, water-ski, sail, watch birds or just relax at one of the lake shore hotels or resorts. The abundant water for irrigation makes the farmlands about the lake highly productive in vegetables and flowers, most of which are exported to Europe. The lake was once an overnight stop for the British Overseas Airways' flying boat service between Britain and South Africa during and immediately after the Second World War.

From Naivasha the main road leading to Nairobi climbs up the eastern wall of the Great Rift Valley and then runs along its edge, giving view after breathtaking view. In clear weather visibility stretches hundreds of kilometres in either direction and down hundreds of feet below to the rangelands stretching along the bottom of the valley. From the road's highest vantage point, a distinctive landmark can be seen—the quarter moon of Crescent Island, dark upon the silver-sheen waters of Lake Naivasha.

Two large volcanoes which antedate the Stone Age, Susua, 7,800 feet (2,357 metres), and Mount Longonot, 9,160 feet (2,777 metres), stand out in the blue-grey haze, the Space Age dish antennae of the Longonot earth satellite station incongruously nestled between them. Longonot peak, now a national park, is a

Below: Giant groundsel in vivid bloom flower only once in every 20 years. From 12,000 foot heights of Aberdare National Park the Laikipia Plains stretch into infinity.

Opposite: Ice cold water cascades over Queen's Cave Waterfall in Aberdare National Park. Giant alpines at left reach more than 20 feet high.

vista of rim and crater. From the old, now little used, road down below on the valley floor, it is possible to follow a footpath from Longonot railway station which leads up to the rim: it takes about ninety minutes for the fittest to reach the top and a good three hours to walk around the knife-edge rim.

Hot-air blow holes exist in the crater and several miles away beyond "Hell's Gate" at ol Karia hot springs have been harnessed in Africa's first geothermal project to provide much of the electric power now used in Nairobi. Hell's Gate, with its challenging 600-foot (180-metre) cliffs and the solitary rock obelisk of Fischer's Tower, offers rigorous tests for rock climbers and there is a wealth of avian life, including nests of the Lammergeier, or bearded vulture, for the bird lover to spot. All this area lies within Kenya's newest National Park.

Once up the steep escarpment, the main road heads south-west from the Rift and descends towards Nairobi, through rich farmland around Limuru and Tigoni. Kenya's first major tea and coffee plantations were established here just after the turn of the century, and now these crops form the highest single source of foreign exchange for the country.

There is a marked difference in the flavour of *robusta* which forms the bulk of the world's coffee, and that of *arabica*, grown primarily in Kenya and in Latin American countries such as Costa Rica and El Salvador. Kenya's *arabica* is regarded as the "liqueur of coffees" and fetches premium prices at the Tuesday sales in the auction hall of the Kenya Planter's Co-operative Union in Nairobi's Haile Selassie Avenue.

There are 10 different grades and many of the deliveries to the KPCU are upgraded by a "magic eye" sorting machine which sniffs out bad berries, known as "stinkers", through the use of ultraviolet light.

Each week a shrewd audience of experienced coffee-tasters, buyers and blenders sits with Coffee Board experts and bids for various grades and quantities of dried coffee cherries sold in lots made up of 50-kilogramme bags. During the 1977 coffee boom the clamour and drama in this hall was astonishing. Auctioneer George Njagi knocked down lot after lot as coffee prices climbed every hour on the world market following a disastrous frost in Brazil. On one amazing morning, in three hours, the lots auctioned raised more than £7 million. Since independence, Kenya tea also has had a remarkable success story, and in recent years the country has been consistently among the world's top tea producers, attaining the highest prices ever recorded at the end of 1983, when India suspended its tea exports temporarily.

Left: Eroded slopes of 9,109 foot high Mount Longonot National Park descend from its knife-edge crater rim.

Below: Flamingos take to the air from Lake Nakuru's algae rich alkaline waters.

The Lakes and the Desert

Intensive farming on smallholdings and large-scale development projects are transforming much of rural Kenya, and the sense of being "away from it all" is rapidly vanishing from many of the areas within easy reach of Nairobi. Yet there is one large region which has experienced little of the impact of modern civilization—the great expanse of the drylands in Kenya's far north.

Several routes lead to a desert adventure, including one heading north-west from Nairobi down an escarpment and along the Rift Valley floor for 80 kilometres (50 miles) before climbing back up the Rift's eastern wall to the western rim of the Laikipia Plateau. Along the valley floor is the small farming centre of Gilgil, close to the alkaline Lake Elmentaita. On occasions this lake hosts a multitude of flamingo—pink and white against a background of dull green waters.

The land about Elmentaita is still largely owned by Delamere Estates, founded by the most flamboyant of Kenya's first white settlers, a Cheshire peer, Hugh Cholmondeley, third Baron Delamere. He set eyes on highland Kenya in November 1897 and immediately fell in love with it. He devoted his life and much of his health and wealth towards establishing modern farming methods in Kenya. The story of his pioneering struggle to introduce pedigree European breeds of animals and crops into Kenya is vividly recounted in Elspeth Huxley's biography *White Man's Country*. Today, it is accepted that Delamere is the founding father of Kenya's sophisticated agricultural industry—his example of persistence, in the face of crushing odds, an inspiration to the millions who now earn their living from the land.

Overlooking Elmentaita is Kariandus, a carefully-preserved prehistoric site alongside a small factory which mines and processes diatomite, the remains of microscopic aquatic life deposited when this area was under an extensive lake. As a fine white powder, diatomite is used in making water filters and paints. Once again, the juxtaposition of a modern industry almost on top of a prehistoric site where man's first stone tools lie scattered, emphasises the continual contrasts of Kenya.

A few miles further along the Rift Valley is Nakuru, once known as the farming capital of the Kenya Highlands and now the country's fourth largest town. Close by is the lake from which it takes its name. Like Elmentaita, Nakuru lake is highly alkaline, and the name, in fact, is a distortion of the Maasai word Enakuro: "the place of swirling dust", an odd name for a lake, but an apt one! Several times this century the waters have receded into a small puddle, leaving the greater part of the lake bed exposed. Winds blowing across it pick up the light alkaline dust and deposit it miles away. During the last "dry-up" in 1954–55, Nakuru town was smothered in an unpleasant white smog almost every afternoon. Happily, only six years later, exceptional rains filled the lake basin and it has remained high ever since.

The sudden rise in the water level stimulated the vast production of the algae on which lesser flamingo feed and which helps to give them their delicate pink colour. The flamingo congregated there by the million during the 1960s, and counted as an unsurpassed wildlife spectacle of the world. A National Park was established there to protect the flamingo flocks and today the lake and its

Opposite: Nile crocodile basks on sandspit in Lake Turkana's Alia Bay.

surrounds contain a wide variety of wildlife. In the 1970s, conditions changed and the flamingo dispersed. However, early in the 1980s, these magnificent birds once again began to assemble in large numbers on Lake Nakuru's waters.

Nakuru is pleasantly situated between the lake and the outer wall of the Menengai Crater, whose 89-square-kilometre (34-square-mile) caldera is one of the largest in the world. On its other side, the road points straight like an arrow down to the Rift floor, leaving behind the pastoral delights of Subukia, a veritable Shangri-la of prosperous farms and secret valleys to the south-east. These fields, plentiful with coffee, tea and vegetables, look out over the magnificent Lake Bogoria, formerly Hannington, from an escarpment wall that rises a sheer 2,000 feet (600 metres) out of the water. On its western shore a turbulence of hot springs and flamingo provide hours of entertainment.

Less than an hour's drive beyond is Lake Baringo, rich brown in colour, its waters usually dotted with the colourful Njemps fisherfolk in their frail coracle-like craft, made from buoyant balsa-like poles, lashed together. The Njemps are cousins of the Maasai who long ago abandoned pastoralism to take up fishing. More than 400 species of birds have been recorded around the lake and bird viewing is a regular attraction. Nearby are two old British forts and the snake farm of Jonathan Leakey, where another attraction for visitors is watching poisonous species being "milked" of their venom, for a snake-bite antidote. Baringo is the end of a smooth well-travelled road. Beyond is Kenya's far north, where the roads disintegrate into tracks, or disappear altogether.

The way north from Baringo runs through harsh, spectacular scenery along the Rift floor, ending in some of the most hostile country in all Kenya—the Suguta Valley. Only the most intrepid will tackle this route wending through boulder-strewn ravines, far from any large centres.

A much easier way to reach Kenya's desert country is from Nairobi to Maralal, by way of Nyahururu, formerly Thomson's Falls. This town, which stands on the lower northern reaches of the Aberdares at 7,738 feet (2,359 metres), takes its name from the cascade formed as the Ewaso Narok River plummets 237 feet (78 metres) down a sheer rock face and leaves the cliffs cloaked in perpetual mist. Thomson's Falls Lodge is set into the forest overlooking this spectacular natural feature.

Over the hills and forest to the east of the Falls lies the Laikipia Plateau with many ranches devoted to beef and sheep production. Some are owned by millionaires and kept more as private game sanctuaries than for domestic stock.

Other large-scale ranches are now divided into smallholdings, where wheat, sunflower and maize spring up in the wake of the rains. A walk across these farms only a few miles north of the Equator is invigorating even in the heat of noon, the air always sharp and clear. Plumes of smoke rise from the thatched roofs of the homes on these shambas and the chickens and pi-dogs keep busy with their flutterings and scratchings.

To the north lies the ranching village of Rumuruti. From here a road runs out of Laikipia into the lands of the Samburu tribe. Close cousins of the Maasai further south, the 70,000 or more Samburu

Above: Alluvial wind blown wastes of Koobi Fora, a 'Cradle of Mankind' in Sibiloi National Park, Lake Turkana, where fossil remains dating back more than a million years have been discovered.

Left: Turkana girl at water hole in dried up river bed.

Opposite: Gabbra camel train treks across the stony wastes of the Plain of Darkness, the Dida Galgalu Desert of northern Kenya.

speak the same tongue and dress in similar fashion. Their administrative centre is the town of Maralal on the flank of a mountain of the same name. This vantage point looks across the lowlands to the Mathews (ol Doinyo Lengeyo), 8,650 feet (2,375 metres), and Ndoto, 8,650 feet (2,637 metres), mountain ranges, oases of montane coolness and forest in an inhospitable region. From Maralal one road winds eastwards to join the "Great North Road" from Nairobi after it passes through Isiolo. Another heads yet further north—a rough track suited to four-wheel drive vehicles only—to Baragoi, Mount Nyiru, 9,030 feet (2,752 metres) and on to that inland sea, Lake Turkana. Beneath the looming mass of Mount Nyiru, this route passes through the "town"—just a few shanties—of South Horr.

The Samburu are a breakaway group of the larger Maasai tribe who chose to live independently in this region 200 to 300 years ago. Their marriage and circumcision ceremonies and much of their culture are very similar to those of the Maasai (who call their Samburu cousins "the butterfly people"). Diviners and medicine men, *laibons*, are highly respected in this pastoral community, which is more and more being swept into the mainstream of modern Kenya society. Many of their traditional ceremonies will soon fade, never to be revived.

The Samburu are essentially a cattle people, with the bulk of the tribe concentrated on the Leroghi Plateau, where they graze their large herds. From the edge of the 6,000-foot (2,000-metre) escarpment the view stretches down to the forbidding volcanic barriers which march through the desert.

Kenya's arid and semi-arid north is a land to stir the senses and test the body. For the most part the land is low-lying, featureless and trackless—at least where vehicles are concerned. Permanent habitations are few and far between—an occasional trading store or mission station, close to the few meagre sources of permanent water, usually wells. Life is relatively cheap, and respect for formal government limited. Raids and stock thefts are frequent. Much of the eastern part of Kenya's desert country was a battleground for bands of Somali "shifta" guerrillas who fought to have much of north-eastern Kenya secede and become part of a "Greater Somalia" in Kenya's first years of independence. The main administrative centres—Moyale on the Ethiopian border astride the "Great North Road", also Wajir and Mandera close by the Somali border—have something of a *Beau Geste* air about them, with their castellated Foreign Legion-style "forts". Incongruously, Wajir, far from the sea, has the Royal Wajir Yacht Club, a fictitious "club" conjuring up visions of blue ocean and swelling spinnakers. It merited the "Royal" prefix when it once entertained a member of Britain's Royal Family. These days the premises form a civil service hostel.

Water has always been the critical problem in Kenya's arid north. Long before Independence, a far-fetched scheme was proposed to drive an underground tunnel through the hills and mountains of western Kenya to irrigate the potentially fertile regions of the north-east with water from Lake Victoria.

In the more practical 1970s, teams of international experts began to explore various alternatives to provide the permanent water

Above: Land Cruiser raises dust in drive across the alluvial floor of northern Kenya's Suguta Valley. Left: Camp site in Sibiloi National Park on the eastern shores of Lake Turkana.

Opposite: Turkana youngster at Ferguson's Gulf, Lake Turkana, with giant Nile perch that measures his own height.

sources needed to permit development in such barren areas.

Kenya's desert regions stretch from the shores of Lake Turkana in the west to the shores of the Indian Ocean in the east. One of the most outstanding natural features is Marsabit, a 5,000-foot (1,500-metre) mountain halfway along the "Great North Road" between Isiolo in the south and Moyale on the Ethiopian border. Along the route is Archer's Post, now a Kenya Army training ground dominated by the towering solid-rock slab of 6,500-foot (2,100-metre) high Lolokwe, looking like a mediaeval ruin. Shifta bandits sharp-shooting from its summit in the late 1960s held up members of Kenya's National Youth Service—two-year recruits who train for their country with picks and shovels—for months, delaying work on the "Great North Road". This sea of corrugations lurches along through the mission and police stations of Laisamis and near Losai National Reserve's untouched game sanctuary. Virtually unreachable by road, Losai is best entered by taking a light plane to a missionary landing strip. Farther on toward dusty Marsabit, a double-storeyed house at Logologo gives a surrealistic illusion of suburbia transplanted into the ancient, forbidding wastes of the Kaisut Desert.

Marsabit National Reserve provides a welcome respite from the scorching desert heat, enveloping visitors in cool, humid greenery. Born out of volcanic fire, Marsabit's summit is swathed from above by constant mists formed when the warm desert air meets the cold mountain air. From midnight until late morning, virtually every day, Marsabit's immense, ancient forests draw their life from these cold, wet, embracing fingers of mist. Trails wind and climb steeply

through the forest before plunging down on the other side, in violent, rutted, slow-motion switchbacks broken by occasional glimpses of glades dappled with sunlight, visible once the mist has blown away. Every bend holds out the promise of magic in this Eden-like setting. The drama of nature is displayed in a great theatre-in-the-round—the crater bowl of Sokorte Guda. Ringed with cliffs, this natural bowl is lined with great stands of timber, hunting ground for talon-clawed birds—martial eagles, hawks and other African birds of prey. The emerald green grasses which grow on the swamp floor are home to buffalo, elephant and smaller animals.

On the far side of the mountain is Lake Paradise, curved like an eyelid, nestling among cliffs. Here, in the 1920s, Martin and Osa Johnson lived for four years. Great pioneer wildlife film makers, they were among the first to use aircraft extensively in observing African wildlife. Marsabit is perhaps best known to the outside world as the home of the late Ahmed—an elephant protected by Presidential decree.

The Reserve has long had a reputation as the home of big ivory. The first elephant to bring it fame was Mohamed, who reigned through the late 1940s and 50s, when many came to stare at the great length of his ivory tusks. The tusks were reputed to be so long that he had to ascend steep slopes backwards! Not long after he died, a worthy successor appeared, named Ahmed. But as Ahmed grew older he would allow only those who were quiet and well-behaved to approach within a short distance. When a wave of poaching upset conservation during the 1970s, President Kenyatta

Right: Somali camel herd at communal water hole in Kenya's far north.

Below: Somali elder in the red robes which mark his respected status.

ordered a round-the-clock guard on Ahmed. And thus was he protected until he died of old age.

How charmed Ahmed's life had been became clear after his death. When his skeleton was taken to the National Museum in Nairobi, irregularities suggested a bullet was lodged in one of his tusks. An X-ray showed a shattered bullet in the matrix of ivory. It had gone right through his skull five years or so earlier, before the watch on his life had begun. A fibreglass simulation of the ancient patriarch stands in the ground of the National Museum in Nairobi and his domain is now ruled by his offspring, with equally magnificent tusks.

Outside Marsabit town, down the mountain slopes, the Borana tribesmen water their cattle at the "singing wells" the only permanent source of water in the region. Singing as they work, the herdsmen form human ladders to descend as much as 100 feet into the depths and scoop up the water in stitched leather buckets, made of giraffe skin.

At the edge of Marsabit township a sign blandly announces Sibiloi National Park, 294 back-breaking kilometres (182 miles) away across the shimmering, unmarked sands of the Chalbi Desert. Once the bed of a Pleistocene lake, the pale sands of this desert seem to direct the sun's rays in concentrated form at all passing life. Occasionally, after freak rains, the old lake floor is briefly covered with shallow water. Normally, though, only the strange beauty of mirages hints at the waters of long ago.

Yet beyond the Chalbi lies Lake Turkana, a remote, fascinating stretch of water 290 kilometres (180 miles) long and 56 kilometres

(35 miles) wide at its maximum, covering an expanse of 6,500 square kilometres (2,500 square miles). Originally named Lake Rudolf a hundred years ago by two Austrian travellers, Count Samuel Teleki and Lt Ludwig von Hohnel, after the Austrian Crown Prince of that time, it was renamed in 1975. More than 300 feet (100 metres) deep at its maximum, Lake Turkana has an astonishing variety and abundance of fish. For untold years it has been the home of the el-Molo people, once reputed to be the smallest tribe in the world, at less than 100 all told, who eke out a sparse living by fishing. In the past, they hunted crocodile and hippo, a pursuit now banned by Kenya's game laws. They concentrate on the south-east shore around Loiyangalani and only the toughest venture beyond this bay on the eastern shore of the lake. The eastern shores of Turkana are scenically dramatic, but are so barren it is surprising how anything, or anyone, can survive. That the el-Molo and other tribes around the lake do is testimony to their endurance and the strong social and political structures of their communities. Yet it is halfway along the shore—at Koobi Fora in Sibiloi National Park—that significant clues to mankind's first ancestors have been found. These early humans thrived in a much kinder environment. Millions of years ago Koobi Fora was lush and green.

Further up the eastern shore the Gabbra, resilient, desert-dwelling pastoralists, occasionally bring their flocks to graze about the lake's shores and drink its alkaline waters. In some places the grass grows succulent and fresh on the very edge of the lake where the waves lap the stony shore.

Right: Njemps fisherman on the still waters of Lake Baringo in a coracle-like raft made from a kind of balsa wood.

Below: Pokot warrior in the Cherangani Hills of north-west Kenya.

North along this same shore and up to the northern end of Lake Turkana where the great Omo River disgorges its waters from the Ethiopian highlands, live the Merille, or Dassenich. A people now of disparate origin, over the past two centuries the Merille have absorbed migrants and dissidents from a number of tribes, and survivors from the Abyssinian slave raiders who terrorised the region until the 1930s.

A hot wind gusts constantly through the arid wastes inhabited by the Merille, coating everything and everyone with a fine veneer of dust. Yet nothing is richer in colour than the sight of Merille fishermen, naked black skins gleaming in the sun, quivering with alertness as they stand in the prows of dugout canoes, ready to hurl spears into the giant Nile Perch, some of which weigh more than 150 kilogrammes (300 pounds) in Lake Turkana.

The Merille have an unparalleled reputation for ferocity. Author John Hillaby, in *Journey to the Jade Sea*, recounts an episode in which a member of another Kenyan tribe was emasculated by a Merille raiding party. Traditionally a Merille warrior must wear the genitalia of a slain enemy around his neck before a woman will become his bride.

Hundreds of bird species, both migrant and full-time resident, find Lake Turkana a haven. Central Island, a volcano that still smokes, is now a National Park. Cormorants, terns and gulls wheel around its towering 700-foot (213-metre) cliffs. Each of its three craters contains a lake, and one of these was a spectacular crocodile breeding ground for years. Indeed, a visiting research zoologist received a savage wound not long ago when he bathed in that

Overleaf: Rock bluff on 14,178 foot high Mount Elgon, the peak which inspired Rider Haggard's classic adventure yarn, 'She'.

deceptively serene-looking lake!

Nevertheless, the gentle lap of Turkana's jade-coloured waters on the island's black lava beaches sings a lullaby so soothing that spectres of volcanic eruptions or crocodiles are quickly dispelled.

The loneliest and most distant of Lake Turkana's aquatic volcanoes is also the smallest. It was here on North Island that biologist Alistair Graham set up camp to study crocodiles for two weeks in total isolation. He was bitten on the ankle by a cobra just as the vessel that had brought him was slipping away over the horizon! As there was nothing he could do, he sat down and began to record his symptoms in the tradition of a good scientist. Fortunately, the snake had not managed to inject sufficient venom to affect him seriously, though at the time he did not know this.

Across the Rift

On the far side of Turkana, north-west of North Island, lies Lokitaung, remote and difficult to reach. Here Jomo Kenyatta endured seven years of harsh imprisonment after a "rigged" trial.

Fossil wood and ancient gorges around Lokitaung testify to the immense age and the violent geological and climatic changes experienced by this region. Millions of years ago Lake Turkana's waters fed into the Nile and covered a much larger area than today.

South from Lokitaung, inland of Turkana's bulging 56-kilometre (35-mile) wide midriff, is Lodwar, where Jomo Kenyatta spent another two years of detention before he was eventually released.

A major highway which runs through all of Turkanaland now links the Southern Sudan with Kenya. From Lodwar it heads south through the lowland territory of the Pokot. Out on the dry flats that stretch on all sides, the pastoral Pokot graze large herds of stock. However, where the land is more fertile and well-watered, they practise agriculture. Years ago, together with the neighbouring Marakwet people, they perfected an ingenious system of conduits to bring water down from the highland streams of the Rift Valley's western wall to the lower arid slopes. In places these conduits actually traverse sheer cliff faces in the form of mud-and-wattle troughs. Those few still in use are now being fitted with plastic conduits. Since the Pokot take the brunt of southward raids by the Turkana, and also by the related Karamojong from eastern Uganda, they are perforce skilled warriors. Those who die in battle are buried facing the Pokot's sacred Mount Sekerr.

Work on the new road began a few years ago at the foot of the

dramatic and scenically picturesque Cherangani Hills, which rise above 11,000 feet (3,352 metres). These hills and their southern extensions on the Rift Wall provide some of Kenya's most magnificent views. At the Kamasya Hills, which lie like a finger off the wall, poking into the Rift Valley between Elgeyo Marakwet and Lake Baringo, is the land of the Tugen, part of the Kalenjin group. Kenya's President Daniel Toroitich arap Moi hails from here. The administrative centre of Kabarnet, a pretty hill station, overlooks one of the most scenic valleys in all Kenya, the Kerio.

It once had the unenviable reputation of having one of the most tortuous mountain roads in East Africa but, happily, the rigours of the nerve-wracking hill climb to Kabarnet are now a thing of the past. In its place, a well-aligned modern tarmac road winds 35 kilometres (22 miles) up from the Rift floor at Marigat.

The new Sudan road, a more prolonged undertaking, climbs to Kitale from the base of the Cheranganis through Kapenguria, a hallowed name among Kenyans. It was in the small village schoolroom there that the Colonial Government tried and convicted Jomo Kenyatta of managing the Mau Mau rebellion. The school is now a national shrine dedicated to his memory.

Just above the town is the Saiwa swamp whose 4.14 square kilometres (1.6 square miles) form Kenya's smallest National Park. It was created to conserve the country's only surviving sitatunga population. The sitatunga, or marsh antelope, is a very close relative of the ubiquitous bushbuck of Africa's forests and thickets. Its distribution is confined to swampland like the great *sudd* areas of the Nile in southern Sudan, or Lake Bangweulu· in Zambia. In

73

West Africa it also lives among salt-water mangroves. In Kenya, however, it is a rarity. In the Saiwa Swamp the species can be viewed from platforms looking out over the reeds. The sitatungas' elongated hooves allow easy movement in the damp world of marsh and swamp. Should the antelope be disturbed, it is able to hide beneath the water, only its nose showing above the surface. Brazza monkeys live in the trees surrounding the swamp.

From here the Cheranganis rise up in a series of incredible cliffs and escarpments, some as sheer as 5,000 feet (1,524 metres). These precipitous cliffs rank among the most spectacular scenes in a country already endowed with more splendours than most.

At the top, to the west rises the 14,178-foot (4,321-metre) massif of yet another of Kenya's extinct volcanoes—Mount Elgon. Its highest point is well above the limits of tree growth. The mountain dominates the Kenya–Uganda border.

This area of Kenya, west of the Rift and south of Turkana, forms a block of relatively high ground, for the most part blessed with good rainfall and fertile soils. It thus contains a very large proportion of the country's arable land and is densely populated. Between the north-west foot of Mount Elgon and the top of the escarpment, the produce from coffee plantations, mixed farming enterprises and fruit orchards finds its way to Kitale, a busy agricultural town and rail terminus.

South, the Cheranganis merge into the highlands of Elgeyo-Marakwet which, in turn, connect through Timboroa and Oldeani to the Mau Range which rises 10,165 feet (3,098 metres) above sea level at its highest point.

Overleaf: Sculpted shapes of an immaculate large-scale tea plantation in Kenya's fertile tea hills around Kericho.

The southern side of the Rift's west wall leads across rolling plains where, at the turn of the century, there roamed large herds of game. Now they have been replaced by extensive wheat and maize farms ploughed out of the ground by white settlers, many of whom migrated from South Africa during the first half of the century. Their pioneering spirit turned Uasin Gishu into Kenya's first "granary". Today, now tilled by African farmers, this is still the case—a failure in the rains on Uasin Gishu can spell trouble for all of Kenya. Its centre is the farm town of Eldoret. Like other urban centres in the country, it has expanded its economic base through a variety of industrial activities and provides much alternative employment to agriculture.

West of Kitale, between Eldoret and the Uganda border post of Malaba, runs a leg of the great Trans-African Mombasa-to-Lagos Highway, skirting Elgon's lower slopes, passing through several small trading outposts serving the farming communities about them. An exception is Webuye. Its proximity to the forested areas of the Nandi Escarpment and lower Mount Elgon made it an ideal location for a pulp mill and an associated paper-making industry. Finance from the World Bank and expertise from Indian entrepreneurs made the development possible and now a town has grown up around this industrial complex—all in the astonishing space of 10 years.

From Webuye it is not far to Kakamega, provincial administrative centre for the Luhya people. Bantu speakers, the Luhya consist of some 17 separate groups all speaking the same tongue. This territory includes some of the most densely-populated land in

Kenya and extends from the slopes of Mount Elgon to the land of the Luo on the shores of Lake Victoria. Gold was discovered in the area during the 1930s and for a short spell Kakamega's wealth and future seemed assured. However, the gold yield was relatively small and the town soon settled back into the less glamorous role of an administrative and agricultural centre.

Close by the town is the Kakamega Forest, the easternmost outlier of the Ituri, or Congo Basin, type of rain forest. The plant species and many of its birds, mammals, reptiles and insects are very different from those in the rest of Kenya. This uniqueness is of particular interest to conservationists and also makes Kakamega a great favourite with ornithologists, who can add many of West Africa's forest birds to their "spotting" lists—without having to leave Kenya.

East of Kakamega live the Nandi tribe, all farmers and stockmen, who are members of the Kalenjin group. The Nandi were the most militarily competent of all the local people and forcibly opposed white rule around the turn of the century and violently disrupted work on the Uganda Railway at the same time.

It is the Nandi Hills and Mau Summit which divide, rather like an arched backbone, east and west Kenya. Nestling in the richly-forested hills of the Mau Range is Molo. Its surrounding downlands are regarded as the best wool sheep country in Kenya. The association between Molo and sheep is to be seen on many of Kenya's menus—whether authentic or not—for the choice dish is often labelled as delectable "Molo lamb".

Around Molo and for great distances away, both north and south

along the high ground, a great deal of wheat is grown. When the first white man entered Kenya much of this highland zone was sparsely inhabited by forest hunters and Maasai herders, or was virtually empty. The temperate climate attracted the newcomers, who rapidly settled in the area. After Independence many white farmers sold out and today Molo is mostly populated by enterprising Kikuyu and some Kalenjin.

From the top of Mau Summit, the traveller heads west towards the vast shallow depression which holds the waters of the world's second largest freshwater lake, Victoria, and its biggest port, Kisumu. The road winds through farm and forest land, undulating but losing little altitude until it reaches Kericho, the tea-growing capital of Kenya. Unlike the smallholdings that produce so much tea in Kikuyuland and Meru, Kericho is the territory of the great tea companies and their large plantations. Organisations like Brooke Bond and the African Highlands Produce Company of James Finlay, representing massive investments of foreign capital, own estates carved out of the forests that still cover much of the Mau Range's western slopes. The largest forest in the nation is the south-west Mau Forest Reserve. Tea here is grown in the plantation style that originated in India and Sri Lanka. The climate is particularly favourable—the high altitude providing the right temperature and the proximity of Lake Victoria ensuring a consistently high rainfall. The daily weather pattern around Kericho is remarkably predictable. Bright and cloudless mornings give way to massive cloud build-ups about midday, which evolve into heavy thunderstorms in the afternoons and evenings. Rain

Above: Lions are phenomenal lovers often copulating as much as forty times a day for several days at a time. Right: Lions are basically lazy and prefer to let the lioness do the hunting.

Opposite: Tourists drift over Maasai Mara's spectacular wildlife in a hot-air balloon.

falls on an average of 335 days a year.

From Kericho the road drops down the flank of the Nyando Valley. Approaching the lake the high rainfall persists, but as altitude diminishes, temperatures rise until the environment becomes ideal for sugar production. The rich green swathes of tea in the Kericho highlands are replaced by the lighter green and coarser textures of sugar cane. Its production is underpinned through great estates and large-scale capital investments. In recent years the Government has sought to repeat the successes of smallholder tea by encouraging similar growth of sugar cane by peasant farmers as a cash crop. This is then bought and processed through the established mills. The "outgrower" scheme shows promise and is indicative of Kenya's pragmatic policy of trying to combine the benefits of both large and small-scale cash crop production.

Kisumu stands at the mouth of the Nyando Valley, close to where the Nyando River empties into Lake Victoria's Winam Gulf. Like Nairobi, this town owes its position to the Uganda Railway. Originally, it was called Port Florence, for it was here that Florence Preston, wife of the railway engineer Robert Preston, hammered home the last line of the railway in December 1901.

As a rail terminal, steamers from here carried material further west to destinations across Victoria's broad waters, the source of the White Nile. Although much of the lake's inflow comes off the highlands of western Kenya, most of the lake is divided between Uganda and Tanzania. The largest river flowing into the lake is the Kagera, which originates in Burundi.

Overleaf: More than a million wildebeest migrate annually from the dry south of the Serengeti to the Maasai Mara's rich grasslands.

Kisumu is Kenya's third largest centre, with a population of about 200,000. Its role as a transport entrepôt has progressively declined over the years, first when the railway to Uganda by-passed Kisumu by looping round the north shore of Victoria and going directly to the Ugandan city of Kampala and, more recently, with the collapse of the East African Community and Tanzania's closure of its borders with Kenya. Now happily trade links have been restored and the earlier setbacks have been offset by Kisumu's growth as an industrial centre, servicing the large communities about the Victoria basin. The city is also the "capital" of the Luo tribe, one of the largest ethnic groups in Kenya. Speaking Dholuo, a widespread Nilotic language, these pastoral people migrated into Kenya from the upper Nile Valley around the 15th century. They gradually adapted to agriculture to supplement their traditional fishing. Today they are numerous in Kenya's trade union movement, provide a great deal of Kenya's industrial and plantation labour and are prominent teachers and academics. The tribe is jocularly referred to by many other Kenyans as the "fish-eaters", a soubriquet earned through their early involvement with the rich fisheries of Lake Victoria and their undimmed enthusiasm for fishing.

It is widely known that, wherever fish are to be caught in East Africa, there the Luo will go to catch them. Thus there are Luo fishermen in southernmost Tanzania, in the swamps of Lake Kioga in Uganda, all around Lake Turkana, and even at water holes and streams in the hinterland of the coastal regions and in the lakes close to Tsavo West National Park.

Closely allied to their involvement with fish and fishing is Luo skill as watermen and boat builders. When the Arab slavers came to the great inland waters, they set about making boats to cross them. They applied the technologies prevailing along the East African coast and as a result of this early influence—and of subsequent contact between the Luo and the Indian Ocean shore—the Winam Gulf is now a stronghold of lateen-sailed dugouts and boats. The sight of Luo fishing fleets setting sail on Victoria's deep blue waters is reminiscent of the long-gone era when fleets of Arab merchants set out to trade, conquer and spread their faith and cultures.

It is possible to go south from Kisumu along lake shore roads, or sail across the Winam Gulf. Aboard the small Kenya Railways launch, m.v. *Alestes*, the new, white high-rise offices of Kisumu soon fall astern. Heavily-laden lighters carrying cargo from Kendu Bay to Kisumu pass by in great clouds of black smoke. Lateen-sailed dugouts lie becalmed, their crews tending nets or sleeping until the wind rises again. Water-borne traffic is still cheaper here than road transport.

On the foredeck of the *Alestes*, fish traders lay out neat rows of "omena" for sale at their destination or to passengers. Silvery, and scarcely the length of a finger, "omena" swarm in their millions after dark around lights held over the water. Thence they are scooped up and later dried on the lake shore; very much a Luo delicacy. Homa Mountain towers another 2,000 feet (610 metres) more above the Victoria lake shore which itself is about 3,000 feet (915 metres) above sea level. At its foot are the headquarters of the Homa Lime Company whose agricultural, industrial and building

products are marketed throughout Kenya. *Alestes* calls in at the company jetty and after a short stay casts off again for the township of Homa Bay, some 40 minutes away, destination for the bulk of the 400 or more passengers. West of Homa Bay, where the Winam Gulf joins the main body of the lake, is Rusinga Island, home of Kenya's famous son, Tom Mboya, who was murdered in a Nairobi street on 5 July, 1969. And here on Rusinga are yet more fossil deposits and clues about mankind's disputed ancestry, dating back millions of years.

Near to Homa Bay is the Lambwe Valley Game Reserve, established principally to protect some of Kenya's few roan antelope. It is now being developed as a National Park. It contains a variety of other wildlife including one species not so welcome in Kenya—tsetse fly which carries the trypanasomes which kill domestic stock. There are also some species that infect man as well and there is a residual reserve of human sleeping sickness, sometimes fatal, in Lambwe.

South the land rises to the country of the Gusii (Kisii) people, a very large Bantu-speaking tribe. Their fertile land comes under the influence of Lake Victoria's rain system and produces tea, coffee and pyrethrum. In addition to their farming skills, some Gusii are renowned throughout Kenya as sculptors of soap-stone. The soft stone is mined locally and is easily worked with simple tools. Catering primarily for the tourists, the carvers not only make articles with African motifs, but also chess sets, candlesticks, napkin rings and other utilitarian items. One unusual traditional skill associated with the tribe is trepanning, the surgical procedure of delicately cutting through the skull to perform brain surgery.

Above: Hippos abound in the swollen waters of the Mara River.

Right: Cheetah and her cub taking water.

Opposite: Cheetah disdains the hunch-backed menace of one of nature's 'undertakers', a vulture.

This is a traditional skill carried out with uncanny precision on patients liberally dosed with potent honey-beer, but which they now seldom practise where modern medical facilities are available.

From Kisii, a number of back roads lead to Kilgoris, in the land of the Kalenjin Kipsigis people who are both farmers and pastoralists. A road to Lolgorien, not far from the Kenya–Tanzania border, which turns eastwards over the Siria Escarpment, brings the traveller to the Maasai Mara Game Reserve.

This is perhaps Kenya's most spectacular game sanctuary. With open plains and woodland patches, rocky outcrops and clumps of thicket, the Mara is a northernmost outcrop (and the richest in terms of rainfall and geology) of the great Serengeti ecosystem of Tanzania. Annually, during the dry months, more than a million wildebeest, and similar numbers of gazelle, other antelope and zebra, come into the Mara. The herbivores, of course, are accompanied by predators—lion, cheetah, wild dogs and hyena. Elephant, hippo and buffalo are present, as were rhino until virtually poached out in the 1970s. The abundance of wildlife in the gentle scenery of the Mara makes it the central point in many visitors' recollections of Kenya, especially during the magnificent spectacle of the annual migration.

From the Mara, the route leads north and east through the Narok district of Maasailand. Wheat and barley production in this area are expanding rapidly, as Kenya strives to feed a population growing annually by four per cent.

The Maasai and Tsavo

No tribe in eastern Africa held sway over a greater expanse of territory in historical times than the Maasai. When the white man arrived, Maasai territory ranged from the Umba River close to the coast, to within 100 kilometres (62 miles) of Lake Victoria in the west, and from Laikipia in the north to Kibaya, 600 kilometres (372 miles) to the south in Tanzania. Their lands have shrunk since then, but not by a great deal.

That they were superb warriors and fine military tacticians is registered widely in the folklore of their neighbours. Their self-confidence and pride in their traditions are such that they have resisted change more vigorously and successfully than almost any other group in Kenya. This is all the more striking because the Maasai lived cheek-by-jowl with the most strident advocates of change—the white settlers—but stubbornly resisted new ways. Their opposition is slowly eroding now, as the government persuades them to move closer to the mainstream of the national ethos. Yet some sentimentalists regret the splendidly independent culture of the Maasai, romanticised repeatedly down the years.

Kenya's Maasailand comprises two districts of Kenya—Narok and Kajiado—named after their administrative centres. The first lies in the Rift Valley Province and extends westward as far as the Mara Game Reserve. The second lies south and south-east of Nairobi right up to the Tanzanian border. Drive southwards from Nairobi and one is in Maasailand almost immediately. Eighty kilometres (50 miles) along the main highway to Tanzania is Kajiado, district headquarters and, quite literally, a "cow town". It lies at the southern fringe of the wide, open Kapiti Plains that join the Athi Plains and roll right to Nairobi's doorstep. Beyond

Below : Maasai warrior in finery of his rank.

Kajiado the country changes. It becomes more rolling and broken. The soils change from black-cotton to red, lateritic types and the vegetation is more open acacia scrub. And as the traveller drives south, Namanga Mountain, or ol Doinyo Orok—the "black" or "dark mountain"—rises higher and higher above the horizon until soon at the border with Tanzania the road is skirting its lower slopes. High on the mountain slopes still stand virgin forests. They give the mountain a dark appearance from the distance.

Ol Doinyo Orok dominates the border township of Namanga, on the main artery to Tanzania now abustle again since the reopening of the border. The tourists also pass through Namanga on the way to Amboseli, at the base of Kilimanjaro. The dirt road from Namanga runs along ridges that all point towards the dominant feature of the whole region: the enormous, snow-capped mass of Kilimanjaro. At 19,340 feet (5,895 metres) above sea level, its highest point, Uhuru Peak, is unequalled in Africa, and in the morning, at midday and in the evening its gleaming white snow cap is visible for more than 160 kilometres (100 miles). Kilimanjaro stands out in sharp relief to the shimmering mirages of the dry Lake Amoseli bed; it dominates all vistas, it is the backdrop against which the traveller views lion, elephant, rhino, cheetah and the host of other game that dwell below in the Amboseli Park. Made famous by Hemingway and several Hollywood films, Kilimanjaro, like the over-romanticised Maasai, is the scenic cliche of all African game lands. Yet, as with the Maasai, the cliche is a tribute to its grandeur and scenic splendour. The visual epitome of romance is an African warrior, tall and proud, clad in a flowing robe, spear grasped in his hand, striding across his dusty territory against the backdrop of an

omniscient Kilimanjaro. The topmost rounded dome, Kibo, has a gentleness to accompany its majesty. Yet its secondary peak, Mawenzi, a full 10 kilometres (6 miles) to the east, is a portrait of montane savagery. Its saw-toothed serrations pierce the clouds and make it the third highest peak, 16,567 feet (5,050 metres), in Africa. It seemed in keeping with Mawenzi's forbidding appearance that for ten years rescue workers were unable to retrieve the victims of a 1955 airplane crash on that peak. The mountain held the bodies in frozen ransom.

A broad dirt road links Amboseli with the Tsavo West National Park, skirting the Chyulu Hills, a "new" volcanic range, some of whose lava flows are less than 200 years old. The wooded crests of this range are lush with numerous forested patches. However, no streams flow down them. Their soil is so porous that all rain disappears directly into the earth. Because of this lack of surface water, the Chyulus are surprisingly deficient in the larger game animals. Many species do climb the hills, but because they have to make long treks to and from water well beyond the base of the range, they can browse to only a limited extent.

The Tsavo West National Park comprises 7,700 square kilometres (2,972 square miles) and contains several attractive lodges. The generally low rolling terrain of Tsavo West is broken abruptly by a series of granitic outcrops or inselbergs, the largest rising from less than 2,000 feet (609 metres) above sea level to just under 6,000 feet (1,828 metres), to form the Ngulia Range. At the base of the mount is Ngulia Lodge, where powerful arc lamps illuminate a watering place just in front of the main building, permitting guests to watch the nocturnal comings and goings of a variety of animals

Below: Elephants with young. These creatures have similarities to human society including the young's craving for constant contact with their elders.

Above : Camera toting tourists capture an Amboseli rhino on film.

Right : Glimpse of the lesser kudu.

99

by the light of "artificial moons".

Updrafts caused by winds hitting the high ground often produce dense mists at night during certain seasons and the combination of mist and arc lamps disorients migrating birds flying overhead on their way south from Europe. As a result they are easy to trap and Ngulia has become a centre where ornithologists place numbered rings on their legs and free them again, the better to understand their migrational patterns. Some come from as far north as the Siberian tundra to "winter" in southern climes.

Not far away from Ngulia and near an even larger lodge, Kilaguni, is Mzima Springs, formed from water percolating through the Chyulus porous soils, flowing eastwards in a subterranean stream and gushing out of the ground at the rate of 10,000,000 litres (2.2 million gallons) an hour. The water is crystal clear and hippos, crocodiles and many species of fish are clearly visible in pools below the springs. In one clearing, steps lead down to a large underwater observation chamber, where viewers meet large fishes literally face to face and can watch hippo families treading in stately, light-toed fashion across the bottom, looking like animal astronauts on the moon in an animated Disneyesque fantasy. Underwater Mzima presents an unusual spectacle of strange, silent, slow-motion beauty.

At the south-western edge of Tsavo West lies a jewel at the neck of Kilimanjaro: Lake Chala, its centre bisected by the invisible Tanzanian border. Its greeny-blue waters have a subterranean source; no surface river flows into or out of Chala. The lake contains fish and crocodiles; and how the fish got there is a mystery. The crocodiles originally may have crawled from the nearby Lume

Overleaf: Ice-clad dome of 19,340 foot high Kilimanjaro, Africa's highest mountain, rises out of the Amboseli Plains above a herd of elephants.

River, to be trapped forever in this serene spot. Until recently, its quiet waters were never visited and the deep crater was silent except for the lap of waves hundreds of feet below and the call of hunting fish eagles. However, now the spell has been broken and fishermen, among them the ubiquitous Luo, harvest the rich bounty of Chala.

Close by is the border town of Taveta, surrounded by sisal estates. It was around this area that fierce battles were fought in the First World War: from today's perspective nothing seems more incongruous than to picture white men and their African allies fighting in the shadow of Kilimanjaro to settle an issue that concerned only Europe. For all the incongruity, blood was spilt in abundant measure and men died pointless deaths.

In southernmost Tsavo West, half in and half out of Kenya, is a far larger lake than Chala. This is Jipe, a shallow, reed-filled water flanked on the Tanzanian side by the magnificent, brooding, North Pare Mountains. The lake is an ornithologist's paradise, sustaining waterfowl in abundance and also providing the spectacle of big game coming to the water's edge to drink. It is said that Jipe is changing from a lake into a huge marsh as more and more silt comes down off the cultivated lands above it. The reed beds that now occur in patches all over its surface used to be limited to the lake's edges, and are evidence of its increasing shallowness.

East of Lake Jipe are the Taita Hills, a great granitic block reaching over 7,000 feet (2,133 metres), and home to the Taita people. These Bantu hill farmers run a flourishing and varied agriculture which includes coffee and a sizeable export of fresh vegetables to the port of Mombasa. Their mountain fastnesses

made them a difficult people to subjugate and traditionally they were avoided by other tribes. Beyond the southern edge of the Taita Hills is Voi, and the entrance to Tsavo East National Park—some 13,000 square kilometres (5,000 square miles) of flatter, more arid land than Tsavo West. Few hills break its low profile and its most remarkable geological feature is the Yatta Plateau. This lava flow is the best part of 270 kilometres (167 miles) long and starts far up in Ukambani, towards ol Doinyo Sapuk. Presumably there was once a prehistoric valley down which the lava flowed for more than 200 kilometres (124 miles) before it solidified. Later, the sides of the valley eroded into the present flat landscape and the harder lava remained, standing as it does now, proud above the land.

Most of Tsavo East has never been opened to the public. It is a strange land with an ominous aura. Its very flatness has a sense of the ocean about it—an ocean of grey scrub and grass in which one feature looks like the previous ten and in which it is easy to get lost. To be astray in the great northern flats of Tsavo East is sentence of death by thirst, yet just as sailors love their menacing oceans, this part of Tsavo East has its own strange beauty for some.

Oryx and elephants inhabit the less forbidding southern areas of the park and crocodiles sun themselves on sandspits in the Galana River near Lugard's Falls. Park trails lead to Tsavo East's south-west gate at Buchuma, only an hour's drive from Mombasa and the Indian Ocean.

The Coral Strand

Some say they can smell the hibiscus and the frangipani, the poinsettias and the oleanders, long before they reach Mombasa. The Kenya coast is a world removed from the deserts, plateaux, mountains and plains wildlife beyond its hinterlands. The climate, the people and the scenery are more reminiscent of coral islands in distant southern seas, than the edge of an often harsh and turbulent continent.

Most come to the Kenya coast to enjoy sun, sand and sea, to relax. The water is always warm, caressing the swimmer. It is rarely ruffled by storms and its denizens are generally kind to man. Sharks there are, but not inside the reef barriers that fringe the white strand. In Kilindini Harbour sharks have attacked humans, but these exceptions have been the offal eaters that trail ships coming into the deep water berths from distant parts. The temperatures are warm, sometimes hot, but never unbearable. And the sun shines clear and warm for at least part of the day, even in the rainy season.

For those inclined to goggle or dive with aqualungs, the ethereal beauty of coral reefs is theirs. Over 200 species of exotic fish reside in these waters about the reef, ranging from tiny brilliantly-coloured jewel fish to huge rock cod, weighing upwards of 100 kilogrammes (200 pounds); from menacing moray eels, peering from their crannies in the coral, to squids jetting away in fear. Those who are not so energetic as to dive can find fascination in the large pools on the shore side of the reefs where the waters are lagoon-like in their calm.

There are other attractions. Shimoni, on the coast south of

Opposite : Kenya's coast is an irresistible attraction for millions of tourists.

Right : Kenya coast fisherman with catch in traditional dugout canoe with outriggers.

Right : Bajun fisherman cleans shells on Kenya's coral reef.

Mombasa, close to the Tanzanian border, is perhaps the most popular big game fishing centre, though there are facilities at most other resorts along the shore. For those not afflicted with sea sickness there are dhow trips under lateen sails, recapturing a whiff of Sindbad's time. Inland, for those interested in nature, there is the Shimba Hills National Reserve in which the handsome black sable antelope may be seen, together with elephant, buffalo and more diminutive life. Further north the enthusiast can visit the Arabuko-Sokoke forest, an area that boasts a small antelope, Adder's duiker, that is found nowhere else in the world. At least two species of birds are also unique to the area.

All along the beaches to the north and south of Mombasa are modern, luxurious beach hotels of international standard, interspersed here and there with cheaper accommodation. The palms, the sea breezes, and the life on and off shore make a calm, soothing environment which lures many halfway round the world to enjoy.

There is another aspect here that is equally interesting, yet totally different. It concerns the coast's colourful history, its towns and Islamic culture. At first glance, Mombasa, island capital of the Coast Province and second largest city in Kenya with a population of 400,000, is thoroughly modern—with a skyline of high-rise buildings, the glitter of glass panels in concrete, and the bustle of a large modern port. Yet Mombasa appeared in Ptolemy's maps of the 2nd century AD and a second look rapidly dispels the first impression. The Old Port and coral town of Mombasa on the northern side of the island are time-worn and indisputably oriental

in style. The narrow streets, carved balconies and doors add to the impression of stepping back to the elegance of a once great era and to a fusion of cultures. The alleys are filled with the aromas of spices, the fragrance of coffee and the perfumes of Arabia. From the mosques *muezzins* call the faithful to prayer regularly at the appointed hours. Close by are Hindu temples and Christian churches. The old port still services dhows sailing the East African coast and from the distant Arabian Gulf, although rusty diesel-powered coasters now compete with the lateen sails, thumbing their noses at the monsoon winds that rigidly dictate the movements of the sailing ships.

It doesn't take an archaeologist to discern Mombasa's links with the past and to appreciate its long and varied history. Once a forest-covered island, Mombasa is in a naturally strategic position. This must have been immediately appreciated by the first mariners coming south from Arabia, as would its suitability as a port. The first settlers from Arabia probably arrived somewhat before the 10th century. By intermarrying with local people they developed the Swahili culture and language, and by the time the Portuguese arrived in the Indian Ocean at the end of the 15th century, the Islamic cultures of the East African coast were well established. The imposition of Christian rule was opposed bitterly and Portuguese suzerainty could be maintained only by force. In 1593 the Portuguese began constructing a mighty fort—Fort Jesus—to guard the entrance to old Mombasa's port. Ownership of the fort changed hands several times between Portuguese and Arab and

Opposite top: Modern bridge links Mombasa Island with the north mainland. Opposite bottom: Mombasa's 400 year old Fort Jesus with Mombasa Club at left.

Below: Segeju family on Kenya's North Coast are famed for their handicrafts.

eventually the declining power of Portugal led to its abandonment and reversion to Islamic hands. Today this 400-year-old edifice is still in good condition and serves as a museum for artefacts relating to the coast's history. The record is one of more or less continuous violence—hence Mombasa's other name *Mvita*, or the Isle of War. The past century must rank as one of the most peaceful eras in the town's long history.

Perhaps the best views of Mombasa appear when it is approached from the sea. The great fort stands out amidst a cluster of ancient buildings. State House overlooks the Indian Ocean and this handsome building is complemented by the verdant and beautifully-landscaped Mombasa golf course. Towering above the course is the modern façade of the Oceanic Hotel, and in the background the skyline of tall buildings hints at Mombasa's commercial and maritime interests.

On the road north from Mombasa some 12 kilometres (eight miles) from the town is the giant Bamburi Cement Factory—one of the world's largest cement manufacturers. This concern mines the coraline limestone of old reefs that underlie much of the coastland as the main ingredient of the cement that is exported to countries in the western Indian Ocean and also the Arabian Gulf.

The operation leaves huge quarries gouged out of the ground, which once concerned company officials. Experts were pessimistic about the possibility of concealing these unsightly scars. The saline water table was too high for plants to flourish. Eventually, the company's own agronomist—Rene Haller, a Swiss of determi-

nation, ingenuity and vision—defied the experts and transformed the abandoned quarry ground into verdant grassland, tall copses of casuarina trees and reed-lined pools. In work that has now attracted worldwide attention, Haller rehabilitated the opencast working to create a wildlife sanctuary, a fish farm and a productive source of timber, employing the recent science of agroforestry.

The ruins of earlier Arab-Swahili towns occur at several places along the coast. Most famous of these is Gedi, concealed in forest to the north of Mida Creek. This was inhabited for at least two centuries which saw the construction of several mosques and other characteristics of a relatively wealthy community. Then, quite suddenly, it was abandoned to the forest. Why? No one knows. What is curious is that none of the old chronicles, Arabian, Swahili or Portuguese, makes any mention of this town, although relics dug from the ruins include Chinese pottery as testimony to links with the Far East.

Malindi, 18 kilometres (12 miles) to the north of Gedi, is also an old town that flourished during the Portuguese presence and continued as a quiet backwater until tourists from Europe "discovered" it after the Second World War. It now features several hotels of international standard. A monument to the famed Portuguese navigator Vasco da Gama, who visited once, recalls the earlier days in Malindi.

Far to the north lie the islands of Lamu and Pate, ancient settlements where the old ways stubbornly persist. But on the way to them is an incongruous sight, standing tall out of the waters of

Left: Carefully preserved ruined pillar in the mystical 'lost city' of Gedi discovered in tangled undergrowth some years ago on Kenya's north coast.

Left: Housewife prepares the family meal on remote and sleepy Pate Island in the Lamu Archipelago.

Above: Colourful sword dance is highlight of the annual Maulidi Festival on Lamu Island to celebrate the birth of the Prophet Muhammad.

Right: Lamu craftsman puts finishing touches to a carved chair.

Formosa Bay: the rigs of Italy's San Marco satellite launching station. Kenya is the only African state to have such a station, blasting rockets into orbit from a point near the Equator to further man's knowledge of his universe.

Also visible from the bay is the delta of the Tana River with its tidal creeks and mangrove swamps. Each year when the river floods during the rains the flow patterns alter slightly. As an old channel silts up a new arm is scoured out; and so, decade after decade, century after century, the delta has been constantly changing. Every ten years or so, when exceptional floods come down, the whole delta plain is submerged and when the water recedes it is not surprising to find that major changes have been wrought beneath the raging waters' surface.

In the last century the delta's main channel came out far to the south of its present course, while a small side channel, the Ozi, entered the sea near the village of Kipini. At the century's end a rubber and coconut plantation was planted about the Ozi and a canal was cut to irrigate it. High floods came and when they receded the extra depth given by the canal allowed the Ozi to capture the delta's main flow. Since then the main Tana has debouched into the Indian Ocean near Kipini.

Lamu Island cannot be reached by car or aeroplane. Only one motor vehicle, the District Commissioner's, is permitted on the island; the airstrip is on nearby Manda Island. The island is a 15-minute boat ride from the roadhead on the mainland, or a five-minute boat ride from Manda's airstrip.

Lamu town is perhaps the best surviving example of the architecture that must have been common along the Eastern African coast at the coming of the Portuguese. It is believed that Lamu was first occupied—in common with the entire archipelago of which it is part—about the 9th and 10th centuries. It is mentioned as early as the 2nd century in a manuscript credited to Diogenes. Vasco da Gama's fleets put into the port and enforced their rule. Over the next three centuries there was continual squabbling between the island and the Sultanates of Pate to the north and Mombasa and Zanzibar to the south. Yet the town survived. Throughout, trade with the Yemen, Arabia, the Gulf ports and India flourished. Dhows arrived seasonally to take the island's products—ambergris, mangrove poles, turtle shells, ivory, rhino horn and slaves. In return they brought pottery and jewellery, spices and metals, silks, carpets and fine raiments. Lamu's island status saved it from the ferocious Galla raiders who subjugated the mainland's hinterlands in a swathe from north of Lamu and, at times, even beyond Mombasa.

There have been other settlements on the island. Shela may have preceded Lamu as the archipelago's principal town and still stands with its attractive mosque looking over the channel that separates Lamu from Manda Island. Shela is now a popular tourist base because of its inviting palm-fringed beach and convenient hotel.

Lamu town has a unique charm as a living antique. Narrow streets and sloe-eyed women clad in the *bui-bui*, a black head-to-toe

Left : Little changed in a thousand years, Lamu Island with its quaint narrow alleys and sleepy waterfront resists the invasion of the 20th century.

Below : Remains of an ancient mosque uncovered recently in the lost 8th century city of Shanga on a remote corner of Pate Island.

garment; shuttered windows and intricately-carved doors hiding flowered inner courtyards behind them; more than 29 mosques, the oldest dating from the 14th century; all these add to its mellow richness and make the past tangible. Will it survive in this manner for yet another ten centuries? The 21st century is upon it and the tourists are also upon it. Seeking to capture the beauties and charms that are Lamu, they may well drive history's spirits back into the shades beyond reach.

The mosaic that is Kenya is one of mountain splendour, rich farmland, cosmopolitan cities, ageless tribal customs, Islamic culture, modern industry, tropical lushness, barren scorching deserts, volcanoes, cool lakes, shining coral beaches and the ever-changing drama of wildlife. To travel in this ever-contrasting land is to experience the constant delight of discovering and re-discovering The Beauty of Kenya.

Opposite: Veiled beauty in the all enveloping bui-bui, the traditional Islamic dress.

Kenya in Brief

Kenya: Attained Independence as a member of the Commonwealth on 12 December 1963, after six months of self-government and declared itself a republic on 12 December 1964.

Nairobi: The capital was incorporated as a city on 30 March 1950 by Royal Letters of Patent presented by the Duke of Gloucester. The population is about a million.

People: The 1979 census recorded a national population of 15.3 million, mainly African, growing at 4 per cent a year. Half the population is under the age of 15 and almost three-quarters under the age of 30. There are about 130,000 Asians, 40,000 Europeans and 26,000 Arabs.

Towns: Mombasa, the oldest town dating back to a 2nd-century settlement, is the second largest town in Kenya with a population approaching 400,000. Kisumu, on the shores of Lake Victoria, is the third with a population of about 200,000.

Faith: The major religions are Christianity, Islam and Hindu.

Main rivers: Tana; Athi-Galana-Sabaki; Ewaso Ngiro; Kerio; Mara; Nzoia; Turkwel; and Voi-Goshi-Rare.

Language: Swahili is the *lingua franca* and the national language, although English is widely used in business, teaching and government. About 75 different languages are in use including Kikuyu and Dholuo.

Entry points by land: Malaba and Busia (from Uganda); Lungalunga, Taveta, Loitokitok and Namanga (from Tanzania); Moyale and Todenyang (from Ethiopia); Kolbio (from Somalia); and Lokichogio (from Sudan).

Entry points by water: Lamu, Malindi, Kilifi, Mombasa, Kisumu, Homa Bay.

Entry points by air: Jomo Kenyatta International Airport, Nairobi; Moi International Airport, Mombasa; Kisumu and Wilson Airport, Nairobi (minor airfields).

Railway stations: Nairobi, Kisumu and Nakuru (main). Border railheads at Malaba (Uganda) and Taveta (Tanzania). Other stations: Voi, Eldoret. Branch lines: Voi–Taveta; Nairobi–Thika–Murang'a–Karatina–Nanyuki; Nairobi–Athi River–Konza–Kajiado–Magadi; Gilgil–ol Kalou–Nyahururu; Nakuru–Rongai–Solai; Kisumu–Butere; Eldoret–Leseru–Soy–Moi's Bridge–Kitale; Sultan Hamud–Kibini.

Below: Traditional lateen sailing boats of the Coast fishermen.

Following pages : Spectacular Kenya sunsets at Ferguson's Gulf, Lake Turkana ; Lake Elmentaita ; Kilaguni water hole, Tsavo West ; and over Amboseli National Park. Final page : Sunrise over Nairobi's Uhuru Park.

Parliament: The National Assembly has 172 members, of which 158 are elected in a democratic ballot. The Attorney General and 12 members are appointed by the President, the Speaker by the National Assembly. The life of a Parliament is five years. The President, currently Daniel arap Moi, has executive power and is directly elected every five years. Kenya is a *de jure* one-party state.

Mountains: Mount Kenya (17,058 feet); Mount Elgon (14,178 feet); the Aberdares (ol Doinyo Lesatima 13,120 feet); and the Cheranganis (11,055 feet).

Lakes: Victoria (63,000 square kilometres); Turkana (6,500 square kilometres); Baringo; Bogoria; Nakuru; Elmentaita; Ol Bollosatt; Naivasha; Magadi; Chala; and Jipe.